It Came upon the Midnight Clear

It Came upon the Midnight Clear

Henry F. French

Augsburg

MINNEAPOLIS

IT CAME UPON THE MIDNIGHT CLEAR

All scripture quotations are from New Revised Standard Version (NRSV) Bible, copyright © 1989 Division of Christian Education for the National Council for the Churches of Christ in the U.S.A. Used by permission.

Illustrated by Barbara Knutson
Cover design by Kerry Staehle
Text design by James Satter

ISBN 0-8066-4050-2

Manufactured in the U.S.A.   AF 9-4050

03   02   01   00   99   1   2   3   4   5   6   7   8   9   10

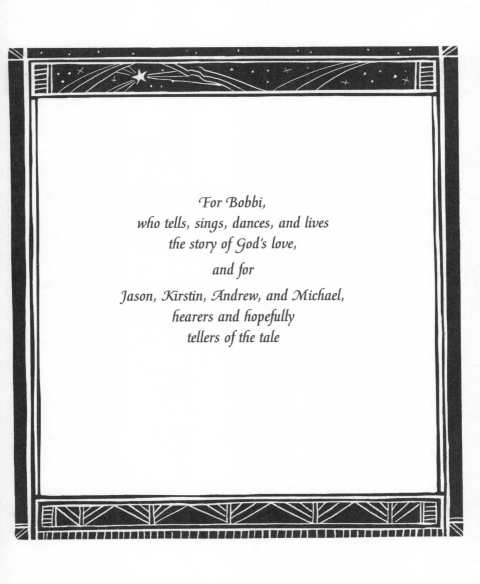

For Bobbi,
who tells, sings, dances, and lives
the story of God's love,
and for

Jason, Kirstin, Andrew, and Michael,
hearers and hopefully
tellers of the tale

Contents

St Thomas Lutheran Church
3800 E. Third Street
Bloomington, IN 47401

Preface

The Christmas celebration marks the beginning of what a Hollywood screenwriter once called "The Greatest Story Ever Told." It would have to be a pretty great story to bear telling for some 2,000 years.

There is indeed something about this timeless story that grabs the mind and heart and soul and fills us with the promise of wonder and the promises of love. And so, in one way or another, we return to the story year after year, filled with a strange longing to hear it again and, having heard it, to tell it to others.

This little book is another telling of that amazing story, along with a few words about the story and about what happens when it is told. It is an invitation to hear the story again and to tell the story, perhaps in your own words, to someone you love.

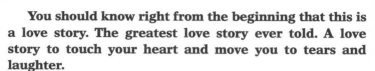

You should know right from the beginning that this is a love story. The greatest love story ever told. A love story to touch your heart and move you to tears and laughter.

All the characters in the story are caught up in the mystery and wonder of love. Sometimes they know this and sometimes they don't. But whether they know it or not, it is nonetheless true. Love touches everyone in this story.

As the story begins, the cast of characters is small. God and an angel. A woman and a man. As the story unfolds, we meet others: the woman's cousin and her husband, an emperor, an innkeeper, many more angels, shepherds, wise men, a king, soldiers, weeping mothers. And of course, a baby.

Years later, when the baby has become a man, more and more people join the story. Fishermen and tax collectors, two sisters, prostitutes, the poor, the rich, both religious people and irreligious people, Jews, Romans, Greeks—all of them a part of the story, all of them caught in the blazing light of God's never-ending love.

The story begins with God. And that is the way it should be, for all things begin and end with God. Which is another way of saying that all things—including you and me—begin and end in love.

Which is just another way of saying that you and I are also central characters in this greatest of all love stories.

Henry F. French

PART I

THE WORLD WAS A DARK, SAD PLACE

Once upon a time,

God cried ...

"*O*nce upon a time . . ." That's the only way to begin a timeless story.

Those magic words bring any ancient story right into the present moment, and "once upon a time" becomes "right now." With the saying of these wonderful words, all the people in the story, and all the animals, and all the strange and wonderful, and sometimes frightening things that happen in a story are right there with you— a part of you, and you a part of them. That's the wonder and the power of imagination.

"Once upon a time," you might argue, is the way to start a story for children. But remember this: We are all children, no matter how old we are, sons and daughters of God, sisters and brothers of Jesus who was born in Bethlehem once upon a time and today.

Once upon a time, God cried. God looked down from heaven upon the earth that God made and loved, and a tear formed in God's eye. God was sad because the world was sad.

God saw that the people who lived on the earth that God made and loved were unhappy and frightened. To be sure, there was goodness and beauty and truth in the world, but it was all mixed up with evil and ugliness and lies. The bad overshadowed the good, and because of all the bad, a lot of people thought that God was angry with them. The world was a pretty dark place.

Looking down from heaven, God saw that what people needed was light—light so they could see that God was not angry at them, so they could see how much God loved them, so they could see how to live in ways that didn't hurt themselves or others.

A great tear formed in God's eye. A great, bright, and shining tear.

In the telling and the hearing of this story, something strange and wonderful begins to happen. The light that grew from the tear in God's eye becomes brighter and brighter, right there wherever you are, in a church, or in your own living room or bedroom, or around the kitchen table. And suddenly, in that light, those who tell the story, and those who hear the story, begin to see who they really are: God's beloved, children of light.

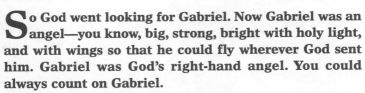

So God went looking for Gabriel. Now Gabriel was an angel—you know, big, strong, bright with holy light, and with wings so that he could fly wherever God sent him. Gabriel was God's right-hand angel. You could always count on Gabriel.

"Gabriel," God called, and God's voice filled the heavens like distant thunder before a summer rain.

With a flash of light, like the lightening that dances around the thunder, Gabriel flew before God.

"Here I am, God," Gabriel answered. "What do you want?"

"I have something important for you to do, Gabriel," said God.

"I'm ready to do whatever you want," Gabriel replied, and then he noticed the bright, shining tear in the corner of God's eye.

"God," said Gabriel, "have you been crying?"

"Yes, Gabriel," God replied, and God's eyes filled with more shining tears.

"I can't help it," said God. "You see, I am in love with the world and the world is in darkness. I am in love with every woman, and every man, and every child, and they are all lost in darkness. And so here's what I've decided. I am going to bring them my light so they can see and find themselves, so they can see and find each other, so they can see me.

"I want you to go down to the earth to a town called Nazareth, to a young woman named Mary, and I want you to tell her what I'm going to do."

"And just what are you going to do?" asked Gabriel, flapping his huge white wings.

God leaned over and whispered something into Gabriel's ear, and Gabriel laughed. It wasn't the kind of laugh that people laugh when they hear a joke or see something silly. It was the kind of laugh that people laugh when they are surprised to find out that something totally unexpected but very good is about to happen.

And that's the way it was. Something very good was about to happen.

Yᴏᴜ might say, *"That's not in the Bible,"* and of course you would be correct. But does it matter? I like to tell the story in my own words.

When you tell the story in your own words, it's OK to make things up, to talk about things like God's tear or Gabriel's laugh. Such made-up things aren't really made up at all. They come out of your own understanding, your own feeling for the story. And the more you tell the story the greater your understanding, the deeper your feeling becomes.

After all, God's tear, God's suffering over a hurting and hurtful world, and Gabriel's laugh, his delight with the incredible surprise God was planning for both Mary and the world—are these not true?

And how do you tell the story to those you love? You could, of course, just read it to them out of the Bible, but I think it's much better to tell it in your own words. Just tell it like I do, as if it were your own story—because it is. The story belongs to God's people and you are one of them.

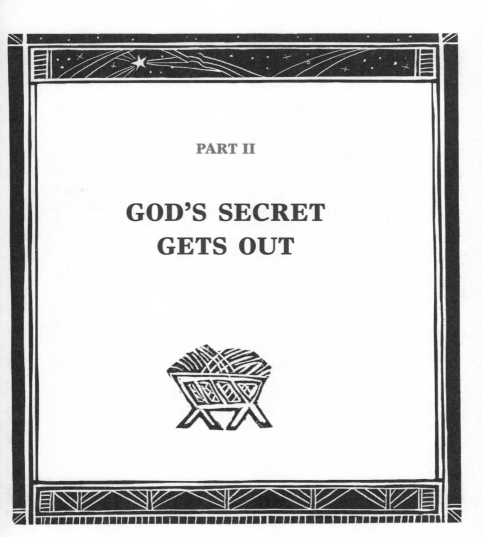

PART II

GOD'S SECRET
GETS OUT

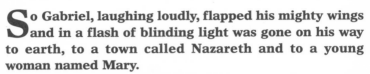

So Gabriel, laughing loudly, flapped his mighty wings and in a flash of blinding light was gone on his way to earth, to a town called Nazareth and to a young woman named Mary.

Now Mary was a delight. Full of life and hope, as all young women should be. She was engaged to be married to a carpenter named Joseph, a strong, good man who worked with his hands and made things—good, useful things, like tables and chairs and cupboards.

Mary was excited about the future, about being a wife and mother, and building a home in Nazareth the way her parents had, and her parents' parents before them.

Gabriel arrived just as Mary was making bread for a new day.

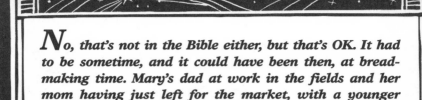

*N*o, that's not in the Bible either, but that's OK. It had to be sometime, and it could have been then, at bread-making time. Mary's dad at work in the fields and her mom having just left for the market, with a younger brother in tow, leaving Mary behind to make the day's bread.

It's the kind of thing that might happen any day. And as she kneads the bread dough, the angel appears.

God is like that, breaking into the ordinary, coming at the least expected times, overtaking the everyday with the surprise of God's presence.

Love is like that, breaking into the ordinary, coming at the least expected times, changing everything. After love breaks in, nothing is ever quite the same again.

Mary almost knocked the bag of flour off the table. There was Gabriel, hovering in the corner of the room, his great wings moving just enough to keep him in the air, his light filling the room so brightly that Mary could hardly see.

"Greetings, favored one!" Gabriel said, a hint of laughter in his voice. "The Lord is with you."

Mary was, shall we say, perplexed, which means confused and scared at the same time, and who could blame her? She wondered what kind of greeting this could be, and what kind of a creature it was who was greeting her. She had never seen an angel before.

I suspect that most of us have never seen an angel before. We go about our daily lives and nothing quite as extraordinary as a Gabriel ever happens to us. Or does it? After all, what was Gabriel but the messenger of God, a word from God, the presence of the divine breaking into the ordinary, the intimation of love.

Has it ever happened to you that at some time—perhaps when you were alone and quiet—you felt a strange presence, a warm and loving presence that seemed to be there just for you? And has it ever happened that in church, or perhaps in a Bible study, or maybe while you were praying or talking with another Christian, suddenly it seemed like a word of greeting, or of comfort, or perhaps a word of warning or command was being addressed to you?

Many are the ways that God speaks to us. Although they may not all have the flash and glamour of a Gabriel, the many ways that God speaks to us, comes to us, embraces us, are all quite extraordinary and filled with surprise if, of course, we are open to being surprised.

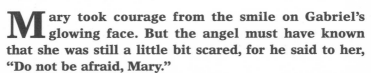

Mary took courage from the smile on Gabriel's glowing face. But the angel must have known that she was still a little bit scared, for he said to her, "Do not be afraid, Mary."

The big angel's voice was surprisingly soft, surprisingly gentle, and Mary felt her fear fly away as if on angel's wings. She smiled back at Gabriel. She wanted to know what this was all about. And so he told her the secret that had made him laugh.

"You, Mary, are going to get pregnant, and you will have a son, and you will name him Jesus."

Well, that certainly surprised Mary. She knew how things happened and she knew that she didn't have a husband yet, and having a husband came first before having babies. So she gathered up all her courage and told the angel just that.

"**H**ow can this be?" Mary asked. "I don't have a husband."

Well, that got to Gabriel. God's secret was so great, he couldn't hold it in any longer. He just put his head back and laughed a great and wonderful laugh, so loud that it filled the whole house. And Mary was so surprised that, in spite of herself, she started laughing, too.

"Mary," said Gabriel, "you don't need a husband! Not a human one. God will be your husband. So your boy Jesus is going to be holy, and he will be called the Son of God. He will be the light of the world and he will save God's people from darkness. In him all the world will see love, will be loved."

God's secret was out.

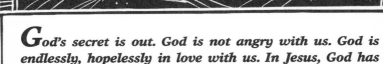

God's secret is out. God is not angry with us. God is endlessly, hopelessly in love with us. In Jesus, God has told us just that in words and in ways that we can understand.

When Mary heard the story from Gabriel, her world grew brighter at once. When Mary laughed at God's surprise, the amount of hurt and hurting in the world decreased, only by a little to be sure, but it was a beginning whose ending is certain.

The last book in the Bible tells what it will be like when the light of God's love that shines through Jesus finally fills the earth. The Christmas story is but the first chapter in this larger story of God's love and salvation.

Death will be no more;
mourning and crying and pain will be no more,
for the first things will have passed away.

REVELATION 21:4

When Mary heard the secret, whatever fear was left in her heart up and disappeared. God was going to do a wonderful thing, and God was going to do it through her.

She felt like she wanted to dance, but she restrained herself. After all, having a baby was a pretty serious thing. Changing diapers and singing lullabies and bedtime prayers and getting up for midnight feedings and the like. A pretty serious thing. Still . . . she felt like dancing.

Summoning up as much seriousness as she could, she looked up at Gabriel. "I am the servant of the Lord," she said, in her most mature voice. "Let it be to me according to your word."

G abriel smiled, nodded knowingly, and in a flash of wings was gone. The room was back to normal, but nothing was really normal or would ever be normal again. God was doing a wonderful thing and God was doing it through Mary.

Suddenly Mary stopped stifling the urge to dance. She moved with extraordinary grace around the room, dancing to heavenly music that only she could hear, singing to herself, "A baby, a baby, a baby! I'm going to have a baby, and I'll name him Jesus."

According to the Bible, the Holy Spirit came upon Mary, and the power of the Most High overshadowed her. What does that mean? What was it like for Mary? What exactly did God do? We don't know.

With the story of Jesus' conception and birth we have left the world of scientific, biological fact and explanation and entered into the world of mystery. Mysteries are not meant to be explained. They are meant to be entered into and lived in.

Telling stories has always been the best way to enter a mystery and discover its truth. Stories invite you into themselves. They invite you into that place where truth is stranger than fiction and is best understood by the heart.

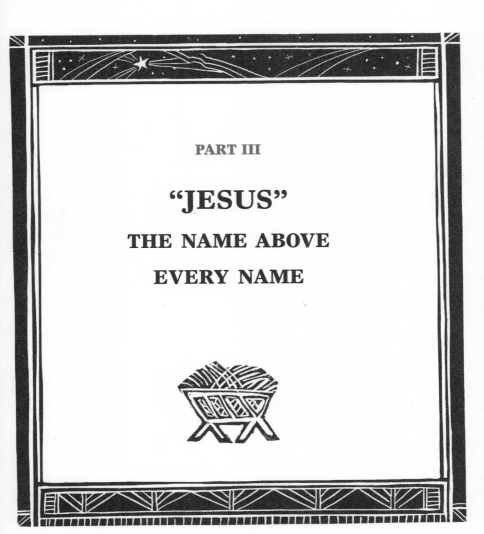

PART III

"JESUS"

THE NAME ABOVE
EVERY NAME

Nine months passed, and Mary's tummy had grown big with the baby growing inside her. She had married Joseph. At first Joseph had been worried about all the strange things happening to Mary, but Gabriel visited Joseph in a dream and let him in on God's secret. All of his fears, doubts, and suspicions disappeared in the flash of Gabriel's wings and the angel's gentle telling of God's secret.

Mary was OK.

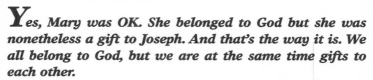

Yes, Mary was OK. She belonged to God but she was nonetheless a gift to Joseph. And that's the way it is. We all belong to God, but we are at the same time gifts to each other.

Mary was the servant of God, but at the same time she was wife to Joseph. Loving God and loving people do not conflict with each other. Quite to the contrary. Mary carried God's child and cared for Joseph, and he for her.

And so it is with us. We, too, carry God within ourselves. For as Saint Paul said, our bodies are temples of the Holy Spirit, the gift of God. It is in the strength of God's gift that we are left in the world to care for each other in the ordinariness of everyday life, just as Mary cared for Joseph, and Joseph cared for Mary.

The trip from Nazareth to Bethlehem was hard for a woman who was close to having a baby. Riding on a donkey is not all that much fun when you have to do it for a long time, and you're not feeling very well, and the roads are rough, and there are no restaurants along the way to stop at and rest. But they had no choice. You see, the government told them they had to go.

The Roman Emperor wanted to tax all the people of Israel without missing anyone, and so he ordered all the people to return to their hometowns where they would be counted and have their names put on the tax list. Joseph's family—which was now Mary's family, too— originally came from Bethlehem, so to Bethlehem they had to go.

It was a long trip, and not very comfortable, but Mary didn't seem to mind. For nine months she had been carrying God's baby. As she bounced along on the donkey's back she remembered the strange visit from Gabriel, she remembered the telling of God's secret: "You will have a son, and he will be the Son of God, and you will name him Jesus, and he will be God's light in the darkness."

"**J**esus." As the donkey clippity-clopped to Bethlehem, Mary kept repeating his name to herself. "Jesus."

She felt the baby kick inside her. For a while she sort of drifted in and out of sleep, still repeating his name to herself: "Jesus. Jesus. Jesus."

They stopped to eat—hard bread and fruit, cool water from a wineskin—and even while she talked softly with Joseph, the name "Jesus" seemed to repeat itself in her mind.

And that's the way the journey went. It was long and hard, but as she gently repeated the name of her unborn child over and over again, Mary felt like God was on the journey with her. She felt that God was within her and all around her, and all would be well. She felt like she was traveling wrapped in God's loving embrace.

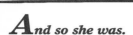

*A*nd so she was.

Something happens when Jesus' name is said, whispered, proclaimed, prayed. The affairs of the world, the affairs of societies and governments, go on. At the emperor's command, Mary and Joseph travel from Nazareth to Bethlehem. But behind, through, under, and over it all God is present, quietly working to accomplish God's will through the power of persuasive love.

At the mere mention of Jesus' name, our attention is narrowed, focused on God with us, loving us, forgiving us, caring for us, blessing us. If you get into the habit of repeating this name above all names, you will get into the habit of remaining focused on God who is always with you. You, like Mary, will find yourself traveling life's journey wrapped tightly in God's loving embrace.

The name of Jesus, you see, is a prayer. It is a prayer that can be repeated at all times and in all places. It is a prayer that expresses in a single word all of our deepest longing, all of our need, all of our hope for today and tomorrow. The name of Jesus: God's answer to the deepest yearning of our hearts.

Therefore God also highly exalted him and
gave him the name that is above every name, so that at
the name of Jesus every knee should bend, and every
tongue should confess that Jesus Christ is Lord....

PHILIPPIANS 2:9-11

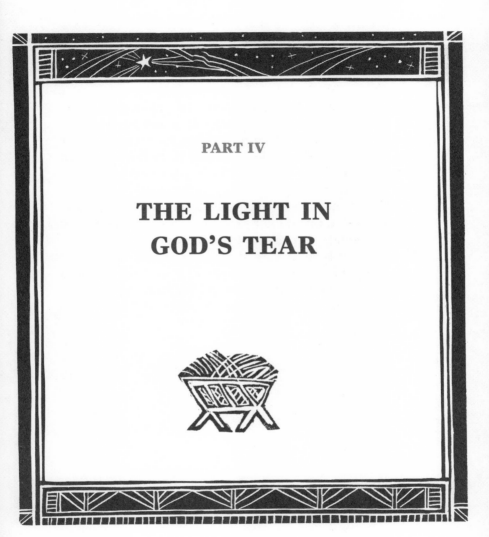

PART IV

THE LIGHT IN GOD'S TEAR

The arrival in Bethlehem was less than satisfying. Road weary and bone tired, Mary and Joseph looked and looked for a place to stay and found nothing. As they searched the city for a room, Mary felt a sudden spasm of pain and knew, in the way that women know, that the time was near.

God looked down from heaven and saw Mary. God felt both her pain and her joy—for in the birth of a baby there is plenty of each—and God's eyes filled with tears again, but this time they were tears of happiness. You see, God knew what was happening and what would happen. Through Mary's pain and joy, light was coming into the world, love was doing a wonderful thing.

A tear of happiness escaped from God's eye and fell toward the earth, and as it fell it turned into a brilliant star that seemed to grow brighter each minute. The star fell until it came to rest in the sky over Bethlehem. And in the light of that star Joseph saw a small, rough stable in the dark, silent streets of Bethlehem. He looked inside and there he found plenty of fresh hay to make a bed for Mary, and a small manger to make a bed for the soon-to-be-born baby.

"It's time," Mary said.

"It's time," Gabriel said.

"Yes, it is time," said God.

Before entering the stable, Mary and Joseph looked up into the dark night sky and wondered at the strange light that seemed to hang over Bethlehem. To their surprise and delight, just at that moment, a shower of falling stars fell from heaven to earth.

*T*hat's not in the Bible either, but it's nonetheless true. Like loving human parents, God weeps with sadness when we are hurt and hurtful, when we stumble about in the darkness of sin. And like a loving parent, God sheds bright tears of happiness when things go really well for God's children. With the birth of Mary's child, things began to go really well for the human race.

*T*he people who walked in darkness have seen a great light; those who lived in a land of deep darkness— on them light has shined.

ISAIAH 9:2

Up in heaven, God heard the lusty, healthy, holy cry of a baby, and smiled. "Gabriel," God said.

"Yes, God."

"It's time."

"Time?" asked Gabriel.

"Time to begin what will never end, the telling of the story. And you, my trusty angel, have the honor of being the first to tell it. In the hill country outside Bethlehem there are shepherds. Go quickly and tell them the story."

"Right away!" laughed Gabriel, and with a flash of wings he was gone. Before a shooting star could cross the night sky, there was Gabriel hovering over the hillside, scaring the devil out of those shepherds. Gabriel, you see, was quiet a sight—especially for folks who had never seen an angel before.

But Gabriel said to them, "Do not be afraid; I am bringing you good news of great joy: to you is born this day in the city of Bethlehem a baby named Jesus, who is the Savior, the Son of God. In him is life, and his life is the light of all people. His light shines in the darkness, and the darkness will not overcome it. This will be a sign for you: you will find the child in a stable, lying in a manger."

And suddenly Gabriel was surrounded by more angels than the shepherds could count, all of them praising God and saying, "Glory to God, and on earth peace to the people God loves!"

Then, as suddenly as they had come, the angels were gone. The sky was dark again, filled with shooting stars. The shepherds were amazed, surprised, shaken, frightened, excited.

"Wow!" they said to one another. "Did you see that? Did you hear that?"

And then one of the shepherds, the youngest of them all, a mere child, said, "Well come on! Let's go to Bethlehem right now and see if it really happened like we were told!"

So they left their sheep on the hillside and went to Bethlehem. They found Mary and Joseph, and the child lying in the manger, just as they had been told. The shepherds stayed for a while. They sat down on the straw beside Mary and Joseph, watched Mary cradle the baby in her arms, and talked about what had happened and about what it meant. They shared their bread and some goats' milk with Mary and Joseph, and then, as the sun was driving the darkness out of the eastern sky, they left.

They were smiling broadly as they walked through the streets of Bethlehem, and if anyone asked what they were smiling about, they told the story.

And in heaven, God smiled a knowing smile. It had begun, the telling of the story, and it would go on and on, until finally everyone had heard the story, until everyone was a child of light, until everyone was enfolded in God's love forever.

Afterword

And so it is. With each telling of the Christmas story, the light that grew from the tear in God's eye gets brighter and brighter until one day all creation will live in the light of God's love.

The story of God's love is indeed a never-ending story. It is my story and your story, to tell again and again. I hope you will tell it often, and in your own words, for the telling of the story is just as much an expression of your love as it is an expression of God's love.

A merry, merry Christmas
to you and yours.

It Came upon the Midnight Clear

1 It came up-on the mid-night clear,
2 Still through the clo-ven skies they come
3 And you, be-neath life's crush-ing load,
4 For lo! The days are has-t'ning on,

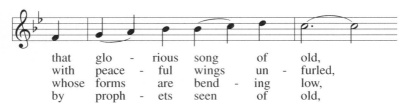

that glo-rious song of old,
with peace-ful wings un-furled,
whose forms are bend-ing low,
by proph-ets seen of old,

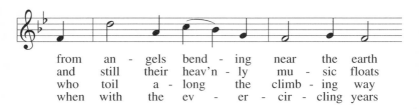

from an-gels bend-ing near the earth
and still their heav'n-ly mu-sic floats
who toil a-long the climb-ing way
when with the ev-er-cir-cling years

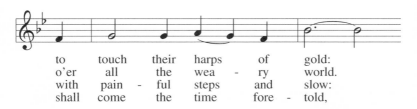

to touch their harps of gold:
o'er all the wea-ry world.
with pain-ful steps and slow:
shall come the time fore-told,

Text: Edmund H. Sears, 1810-1876, alt.
Tune: Richard S. Willis, 1819-1900

"Peace on the earth, good will to all,
A - bove its sad and low - ly plains
Look now, for glad and gold - en hours
when peace shall o - ver all the earth

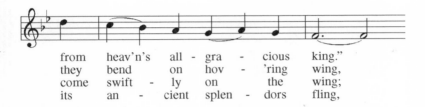

from heav'n's all - gra - cious king."
they bend on hov - 'ring wing,
come swift - ly on the wing;
its an - cient splen - dors fling,

The world in sol - emn still - ness lay
and ev - er o'er its ba - bel sounds
oh, rest be - side the wea - ry road
and all the world give back the song

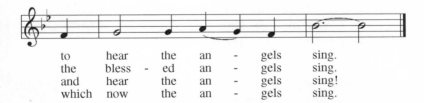

to hear the an - gels sing.
the bless - ed an - gels sing.
and hear the an - gels sing!
which now the an - gels sing.

About the Author

Henry F. French has served the Evangelical Lutheran Church in America as a missionary pastor and teacher, seminary professor, and editorial director. *It Came Upon the Midnight Clear* was first written and delivered as a Christmas sermon in two voices, with Pastor French reading the narrative and his wife, Bobbi, reading the commentary in italics. The annual reading of the story has become a tradition in the French family. You are encouraged to make it a tradition in your family as well.

About the Illustrator

Barbara Knutson grew up in South Africa as the daughter of American missionaries. She later taught in Nigeria and lived for two years in Peru. Barbara now resides in St. Paul, Minnesota, where she illustrates books. Her other books include *Kwanzaa Karamu*, *Hanna's Cold Winter*, and *Manger in the Mountains*.